Contents

Penpal from the Black Planet

14.03.2020

Text from: Zog

(on the Black Planet)

Text to: Rick Scott

(at 41 Cross Hills Flats, Earth)

Zog to Earth! Zog to Earth!

Testing, testing!

I am texting U to ask U if U will B my penpal. It's a bit dull on the Black Planet. It's just black rocks and a lot of dust. I fix up my rocket, and run to the astro-shop for my mum, and that's it. I get a bit fed up with it.

B my penpal! Bring on the fun!

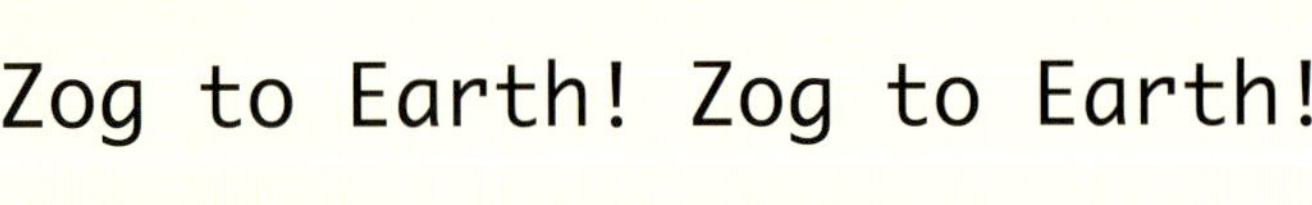

Sending ...

Thanks for the text! A text from the Black Planet! Yes, I will B your penpal. I will send U pics of me and Mum and Dad (and my Nan, and Jess). Oh, yes – and Scruff the dog, and Fluff the cat.

I'm sitting in the flat, with my laptop and my felt tip pens. I'm finishing my maths project (not!). Jess is on the drums – she's in a band.

Mum is getting fish and chips from the chip shop, it's the best! Nan is knitting – she knits for England. She knitted me a hat with a pink pompom, but it got lost – with a bit of help from me!

I go to school on the bus. I'm in Miss Grim's class. It's OK, but Miss Grim's a bit posh.

Must go!

Sending ...

17.03.2020

Text from: Zog (on the Black Planet)

Text to: Rick Scott (at 41 Cross Hills
           Flats, Earth)

I wish I had a cat and a dog! U don't get them on the Black Planet – U just get long wet red things with ten legs and they stink!

I'm fixing up my rocket. It's the fastest thing on the Black Planet! Well, I think it is. I just fill up the tank and then, with a flash and a bang – it's blast-off! But the rocket's lost a fin and I must stick it back on.

Sending ...

20.03.2020

Text from: Rick Scott (at 41 Cross Hills Flats, Earth)

Text to: Zog (on the Black Planet)

I'm glad that red thing is on the Black Planet, and not Planet Earth!

I'm fed up, Zog. Jess is on the drums – it's such a racket! Miss Grim is cross with me – it's my rubbish spelling. (And I had to put my gum in the bin.) Mum nags me – on and on.

I've had it with Planet Earth. Can I visit you on the Black Planet? Will U fetch me in the rocket?

From Rick (V.fed up)

PS The rocket can land on the top of the flats.
Is it fixed yet?

Sending ...

I set off in my rocket to fetch you, but the electrics went wrong and I missed Cross Hills Flats. In fact, I missed England! I landed, with a big bump, in Canada! *And* I got an electric shock!

U Earthlings are a funny lot! I filmed lots of Earthlings on my webcam.

And the things U call animals – well! Things U can sit on, that go "clip-clop"! Fuzzy things that go "baa"?!

Got to stop – a big Earthling with a badge on his cap wants to catch me! Must get back to my rocket – **aaaaagh** – he's got me!

Challenge Prof. the Boff !

This is Prof. the Boff.
Prof. thinks he is king of
the animals!

Think of an animal and Prof. the Boff reckons he has
the facts.

Hmmm ... This will be a bit of a challenge then!
Can we trip Prof. the Boff up? Well, we got Tom, a lad
from Kent, to grill him on wolves.

Is Prof. the Boff the king of cubs? Is he a whizz on
wolves? Is ...

Can we just get on with it?

Prof. the Boff: Bring it on!

Tom: If I trapped a wolf cub, is it OK to have it as a pet?

Prof. : No! But dogs belong to the wolf family. Get a dog and you will
have a bit of a wolf as a pet.

Tom: Gran's bulldog has a bit of wolf in him?
So Gran has a wolf in the kitchen then?

Prof. : Ha! Yes!

Tom: Is a wolf a mammal?

Prof. : Yes, it is a mammal as it has lungs and
when it is a cub, it drinks its mum's milk.

Tom: Just checking. And if I want to spot a wolf,
I go to?

Prof. : Alaska ...

Tom: You will ask who? Your mum?

Prof. : Can I finish? It is best to go to Alaska
and Canada to spot wolves.

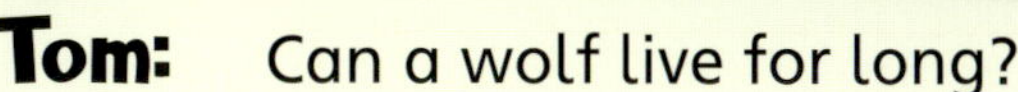

Tom: Can a wolf live for long?

Prof. : Wolves can live to be 10.
The oldest got to 17!

Tom: What can kill a wolf?

Prof. : Illness, scraps with wolves in the
pack ... and us.

Tom: Us?

Prof. : Yup! We hunt and kill them for fun and
when they kill our chickens and pets.

Tom: That's not good.

Prof. : A wolf has a pelt that can be sold as well.

Tom: OK, what's the best thing you can tell me?

Prof. : Let me think ... Well, if a wolf is cross, it will scrunch up its muzzle and flash its fangs.

Tom: And ...

Prof: It will howl to tell the pack where it is and when a hunt has ended in a kill.

Tom: OK, OK, you win the challenge, but I have a wolf gag for you. Knock, knock.

Prof. : Who's that?

Tom: Fred.

Prof. : Fred who?

Tom: Who's a Fred of the big bad wolf?

Prof. : I will do the wolf gags, OK?

Hank Stock – strong man

Bob: Hi! I'm Bob King. I'm standing on Fogg Street in Dallas, Texas. I'm with Hank Stock. He says he's the strongest man in the USA. Is that correct, Hank?

Hank: Yes it is, Bob. I'm as strong as ten men.

Bob: And tell us, Hank, how did you get so strong?

Hank: Well, Bob, I began by lifting things such as sacks of spuds and bags full of sand. Next, I lifted stacks of bricks and big rocks. Then I lifted men.

Bob: Men, Hank?

Hank: Yes, Bob. Last Sunday I lifted six men. Big men.

Bob: All at once?

Hank: Correct, Bob.

Bob: And did it all go well?

Hank: Well, yes and no Bob.

I did drop one man.

Crash! He landed on his back.

Crack! He busted his leg.

Bob: And what will you lift today,
Hank?

Hank: I have a big test today, Bob.

A very big test.

Bob: Will you lift a hut, Hank?

Hank: Huts are for wimps, Bob.

Bob: Is it a truck, Hank?

Hank: A truck? Nuts to trucks, Bob!

Bob: A tank then?

Will you lift a tank, Hank?

Hank: Tanks stink, Bob.

Bob: Then what is it, Hank?

What will you lift today on Channel 9 TV?

Hank: Today, Bob, I will lift a shop.

Bob: A shop, Hank?

Hank: A shop. I'll lift it, twist it and toss it up and down.

I am the strongest man in the USA, Bob.

Bob: This is it. Hank is bending down.

He's picking up Rick's Gift Shop.

He's lifting it!

He's standing still, with a shop on his head!

Hank Stock is a shoplifter!

He's twisting it!

He's tossing it up and down!

This is fab! This is brill!!

But hang on …
He's sinking!

Hank is sinking in the
soft land.
The shop is bashing
him into the mud!
It's crushing him!

Hank Stock

Shoplifter

1980–2009

A big man. He lifted a shop onto his head.

It's still there.

Six top tricks!

Want to be a top prank player?
Okay, have a go at six tricks that will set
you on your way.

Red dots give top prank ranking!

⬤◯◯◯◯ Not bad.

⬤⬤◯◯◯ Okay and not difficult to pull off.

⬤⬤⬤◯◯ A hot gag to play ...

⬤⬤⬤⬤◯ Way to go, prankster!

⬤⬤⬤⬤⬤ Tops for shocks!

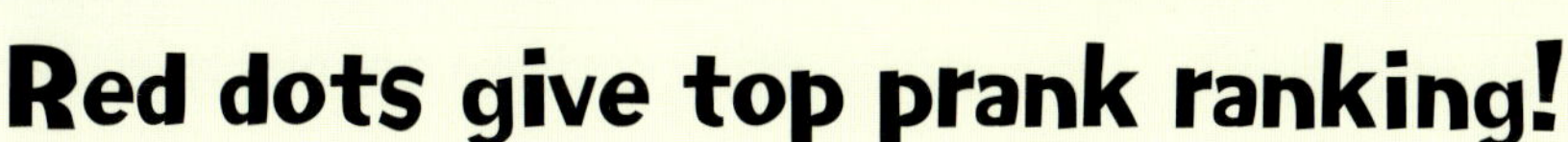

Put lots and lots of confetti in Mum's folded up umbrella. On the next wet day, Mum won't have an inkling that she will get a sprinkling when she puts that umbrella up ...

● ● ○ ○ ○

Say you are off to play with a pal. Mix crispies with a bit of red jam. Slap it on your arm and then run back in yelling and saying that you have cut yourself. Extra yuck ranking if you then lick the "bad cut" away!

● ● ● ○ ○

3. Slip-slop plot!

Cling film – the prank player's pal! Get a glass of milk and put cling film on top of the glass.

When Dad is on the PC, rush in holding the glass, pretend to trip up, (yell so Dad spots you and the drink) and then sway next to him.

Check Dad's dismay as he thinks it will spill on his PC!

Get a dish and ½ fill it with a disgusting mix such as cold mash, jam and bits of sloppy gunk. Then put lots and lots of candy on top. Say to a pal, "Help yourself!" They grab a handful of candy and get an extra helping of gunk they didn't expect!

5. Thing on a string

Okay – this is an old trick but ... Attach an extra long bit of cotton to 50p. Put the 50p on a grassy patch so the cotton is hidden. Check you are hidden away and hang on to the end of the cotton. When your "victim" bends and picks up the 50p, pull it away! A brill trick to play and at the end of the day, you still have the 50p!

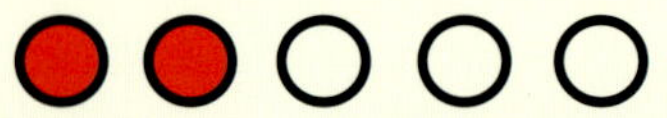

6. The – 'quick, quick I want to be sick' – trick!

Get a thick plastic shopping bag. Fill it with a bit of liquid and cold veg soup from a can (ring pull cans are best). Attach an elastic band (this stops it spilling). Slip the bag up your top so it can't be spotted. Pop to your pal's and say:

I am ill today.
I think I am going to be sick!

And then ...

Clutch your tum, pull the band off and press the bag as you bend and retch.

The veg gunk will spill and your pal will think you have been sick!

May be that they will run away and you will have to stay qand mop it up – but what a top prank!

The day of the dog

8.30

Mr Peel's clock goes off.

Ting ting ting — what a racket!

I was fast asleep! He tells me to get out of my basket

— but I want to stay in it!

A dog needs his sleep, and my green blanket feels *so* soft!

9.00

Mr Peel feeds me.

You can guess what's in the dish — Doggo from a can.

It's been Doggo every day this week.

He has a big dish of choc pops and a pot of coffee

— he's so greedy.

11.00

We set off for the park.

I see the postman and flash

my teeth at him.

I want to nip him on the knee,

but Mr Peel yells at me.

Can't a dog have any fun?

12.00

We're in the park.

I see my doggy pals, and I want to run to meet them, but I have to stay with Mr Peel.

He gets a big bag of sweets and toffees out of his pocket — but nothing for me.

3.00

On the way back to the flat, we call in at the vet. Oh, no — she says I need a jab!

I've never seen such a big needle!

4.00

Next, I get a bath and a trim.

Then the man sprays me with doggy scent! Ugh!

This happens every week!

5.00

Mr Peel pops into the shop.

He gets a fillet of beef, and some posh

French cheese — he's very keen on cheese.

And yes, you've guessed it —

fifteen cans of Doggo, all for me.

6.00

A dish of Doggo, and a drink.

7.00

Mr Peel sits on the settee and watches a film called

'Free Willy'.

No dogs in it.

9.00

I have to do tricks!

I sit up and beg for choccy sweets.

I do hundreds of keepy-uppies with my ball.

(Well, it seems like hundreds.)

I need a rest!

10.00

I'm back in my basket. What a day!

I want to sleep for a week!

Mr Peel's rubbish at looking after a dog!

He can't see how it feels when you have to go to the vet for a

whopping big jab, or when you keep getting rotten old Doggo for

your dinner.

Well, today he is feeling ill —

he's sneezing a lot —

and he's going to stay in bed.

So today is the day of the dog!

8.30

I'm in my basket.

10.00

I'm still in my basket.

11.00

 I'm still in my basket. I've had a long sleep,

and I need feeding!

I look in the fridge.

Yum! Mr Peel has left a big bit of beef.

I pull it out, and drag it to my basket.

I munch away.

11.30

I run out of the flat.

I see the postman, and it's a nip on the knee for him!

Then I'm off to the park.

12.00

I meet my dog pals in the park. Big Ray (the scruffy one) has got the biggest

feet I've ever seen!

We all run across the grass at top speed.

We splash in the pond, and roll in the mud.

We're all wet and smelly!

Big Ray has got pond weed on his back!

No Mr Peel to stop the fun!

1.00

All the lads come back to the flat with me.

1.30

There's lots of black mud on Mr Peel's best rug!

3.00

We have chicken legs for lunch — lots of them, with chips and ketchup. Fantastic!

Big Ray has sixteen of them! There's not much left for Mr Peel.

5.00

Then we all sit on the settee — more mud!

We watch Crufts on TV. We see a

sheepdog with a flock of sheep.

Then a black pit bull wins 'Top Dog'.

We all say 'Wuff! Wuff!'

It's been the best day!

No vets, no baths, no silly tricks —

just lots of grub, lots of pals and lots of mud.

Hurray for the day of the dog!

A penpal on the Black Planet (a e i o u – CVC, CVCC, CCVC words)

Green words: *Say the sounds. Say the word.*

bla<u>ck</u>   bri<u>ng</u>   text   send   <u>kn</u>its   <u>ch</u>ips   <u>wr</u>o<u>ng</u>   from cro<u>ss</u>

hi<u>ll</u>s   flats   du<u>ll</u>   ro<u>ck</u>s   <u>sh</u>op

Say the syllables. Say the word.

pen'pal → penpal   plan'et → planet   fast'est → fastest   ro<u>ck</u>'et → ro<u>ck</u>et

ru<u>bb</u>'i<u>sh</u> → ru<u>bb</u>i<u>sh</u>   ra<u>ck</u>'et → ra<u>ck</u>et   pom'pom → pompom

Say the root word. Say the whole word.

test → testi<u>ng</u>   text → texti<u>ng</u>

Red Words: to   of   <u>are</u>   a<u>ll</u>   want   my*   he*   me*   be*   go*   <u>sh</u>e*   s<u>ch</u>ool*

no*

** These words are red for a while*

Challenge words:

<u>Ear</u>th   E<u>ng</u>land   <u>for</u>   ba<u>dge</u>   astro   almost

Vocabulary check: **astro** *outer space*   **pompom** *ball of fluff, often on top of hats*

Challenge Prof. the Boff (a e i o u – CVC, CVCC, CCVC words)

Green words: *Say the sounds. Say the word.*

bo<u>ff</u>   ki<u>ng</u>   we<u>ll</u>   gri<u>ll</u>   <u>kn</u>o<u>ck</u>   scraps   pet   trip

lad   hunt   facts   from   bri<u>ng</u>   <u>then</u>   gran   <u>think</u>

Say the syllables. Say the word.

ma<u>mm</u>'al → ma<u>mm</u>al   Al'ask'a → Alaska   re<u>ck</u>'on → re<u>ck</u>on   i<u>ll</u>'ne<u>ss</u> → i<u>ll</u>ne<u>ss</u>

Say the root word. Say the whole word.

<u>ch</u>eck → <u>ch</u>e<u>ck</u>i<u>ng</u>   trap → tra<u>pp</u>ed

Red words:

of   to   y<u>ou</u>   <u>wh</u>at   <u>wh</u>o   <u>wh</u>ere   <u>your</u>   want   <u>th</u>ey   he*   we*   be*   no* so*

go*   me*   ** These words are red for a while*

Challenge words:

<u>how</u>   wol<u>ve</u>s   wolf   <u>for</u>   sold   family   <u>our</u>   oldest

Vocabulary check: **muzzle** *nose or snout of a wolf*   **pelt** *fur and skin of a wolf*

Hank Stock - strong man (a e i o u – CVC, CVCC, CCVC words)

Green words: *Say the sounds. Say the word.*

Sto<u>ck</u>　　strong　　ro<u>ck</u>s　　sand　　<u>sh</u>op　　tru<u>ck</u>　　sti<u>ll</u>

help　　ta<u>nk</u>　　spuds　　ten　　Ha<u>nk</u>

Say the syllables. Say the word.

strong'est → strongest　　<u>chann</u>'el → <u>channel</u>

Say the root word. Say the whole word.

lift → lifted　　twist → twisti<u>ng</u>

Red words:

to　<u>are</u>　of　<u>th</u>ere　<u>you</u>　<u>what</u>　<u>all</u>　on<u>ce</u>　he*　no*　go*　by*

Challenge words:

tod<u>ay</u>　　Sund<u>ay</u>　　s<u>ay</u>　　h<u>ea</u>d　　str<u>ee</u>t　　co<u>rr</u>ect　　d<u>ow</u>n　　one

hi　　h<u>ow</u>　　very　　began

Vocabulary check: **spuds** *potatoes*　　　**stacks** *lots of*

Six top tricks! (ay)

Green words: *Say the sounds. Say the word.*

ok<u>ay</u>　　pl<u>ay</u>　　w<u>ay</u>　　aw<u>ay</u>　　s<u>ay</u>　　d<u>ay</u>　　sw<u>ay</u>　　st<u>ay</u>　　m<u>ay</u>

Say the syllables. Say the word.

dis'm<u>ay</u> → dism<u>ay</u>

Say the root word. Say the whole word.

<u>sh</u>op → <u>sh</u>oppi<u>ng</u>　　spot → spo<u>tt</u>ed

Red words:

want　to　<u>you</u>　<u>your</u>　of　<u>are</u>　<u>th</u>ey　<u>what</u>　be*　go*　<u>she</u>*　he*　so*

Challenge words:

<u>for</u>　　soup　　bro<u>ll</u>y　　fo<u>ll</u>y　　crispies　　candy　　fold<u>ed</u>　　pl<u>ay</u>er

cold　　old　　confe<u>tt</u>i　　won't　　can't　　handy　　gra<u>ss</u>y　　slo<u>pp</u>y

li<u>qu</u>id　　holdi<u>ng</u>

Vocabulary check:　　　**confetti** *small bits of torn up paper*

retch *noise made when you are being sick*　　**victim** *someone who will get caught out by your trick*

folly *silliness or foolishness*　　**inkling** *a hint*